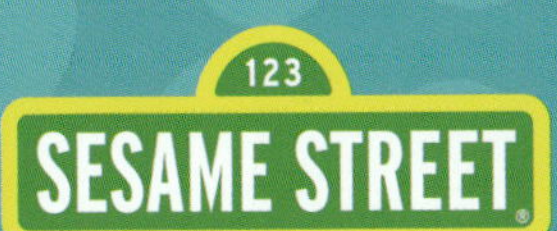

First Visit to the Doctor with Elmo

Patricia J. Murphy

Lerner Publications ◆ Minneapolis

Discover six early milestones alongside your favorite *Sesame Street* friends! From visiting the dentist to getting a library card, this series helps young children feel prepared for new and exciting experiences that are a part of growing up.

Sincerely,
The Editors at Sesame Workshop

Table of Contents

Being Healthy

It's important to keep our bodies healthy. One way to stay healthy is by visiting the doctor!

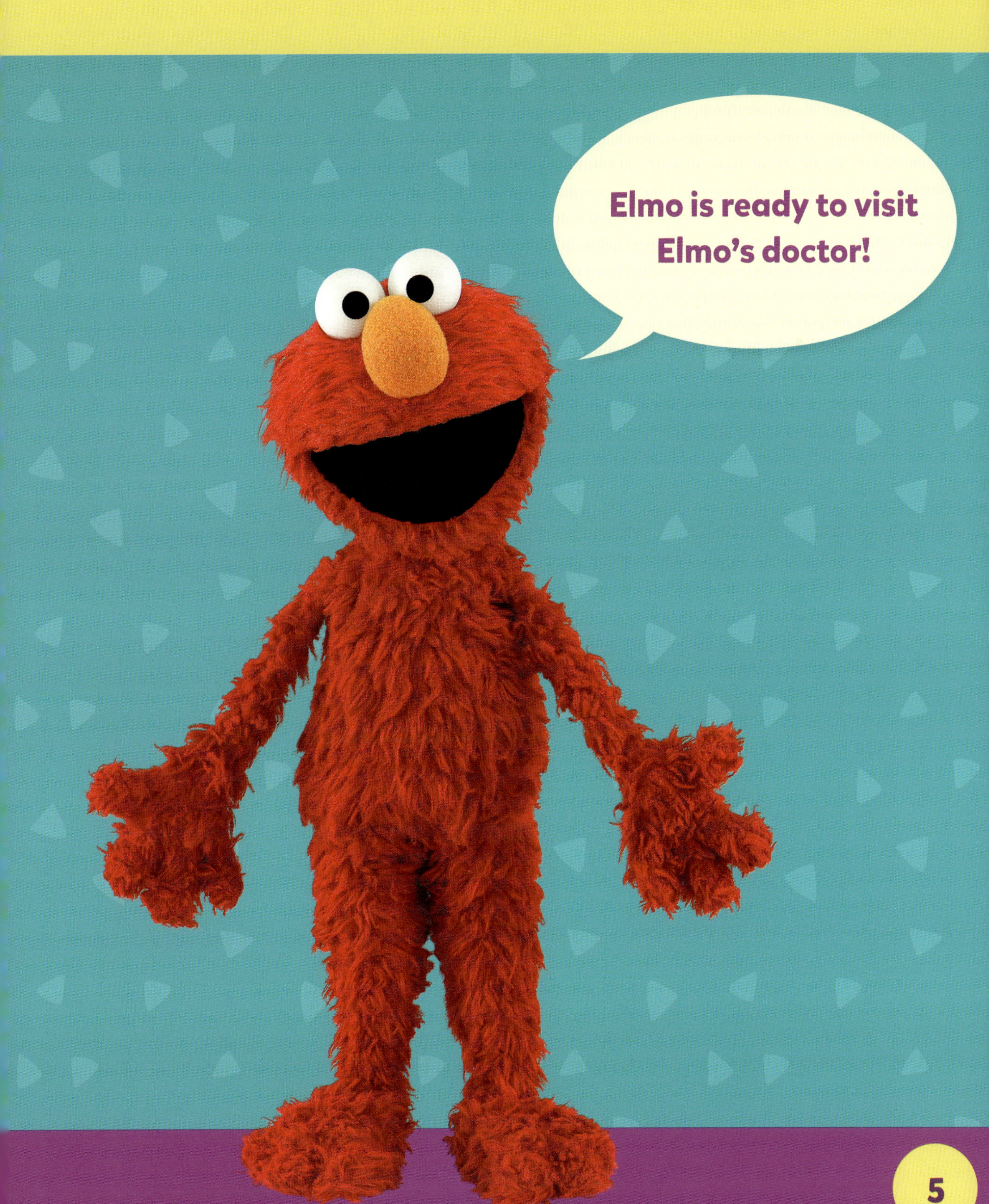
Elmo is ready to visit Elmo's doctor!

Doctor Visits

It's good to have checkups every year.

I see my doctor for a checkup every year around my birthday.

This helps keep us healthy and strong.

At your checkup, the doctor or nurse will check to see how you're growing. First, they will measure your height with a tall ruler and your weight with a scale.

My doctor measures
my height each year.
I'm 8 feet, 2 inches tall!

Next, the doctor will check your ears and eyes. They will use a special tool called an otoscope to look in your ears.

Then they'll use another tool to look at your eyes.

The doctor will use a tool called a stethoscope to listen to your heart and lungs. They will place the end of the stethoscope on your chest to hear your heartbeat.

Then they'll listen to your lungs as you breathe in and out.

Sometimes, the doctor or nurse will give you a shot to keep you healthy. A shot may hurt a little bit—like a pinch. But it will be over quickly!

After my shot, I got
a bandage and a
cool sticker!

When we feel sick or hurt, visiting the doctor can help us feel better.

Me visit doctor,
and me feel better.

You might visit the doctor when you have an earache, a fever, or a broken bone.

My abuela took me to the doctor when I had a sore throat and a runny nose. The doctor helped me feel healthy again.

Visits to the doctor can help us in many ways. We see the doctor for checkups and when we feel sick or are hurt. Seeing the doctor helps us stay healthy.

Get Ready for Your Doctor Visit

Make believe that you're a doctor or nurse and you're taking care of your stuffed animal.

1. **Measure them with a ruler.**
2. **Look in their eyes, ears, nose, and mouth.**
3. **Pretend to listen to their heart and lungs.**
4. **Give a "shot" with a soft touch of a finger.**
5. **Celebrate by giving them a sticker at the end of the visit!**

Glossary

doctor: a person who treats illnesses and injuries and who we see for checkups

nurse: a person who helps doctors treat illnesses and injuries and who we see for checkups

otoscope: a tool used to check the ears

stethoscope: a tool used to listen to the heart and lungs

Read More

Leed, Percy. *Doctors: A First Look*. Minneapolis: Lerner Publications, 2025.

MacReady, R. J. *Going to the Doctor*. New York: Cavendish Square, 2022.

Schuh, Mari C. *Dana's Visit to the Doctor*. Minneapolis: Jump!, 2023.

Photo Acknowledgments

Image credits: FatCamera/Getty Images, pp. 3, 8, 12, 16; Drazen Zigic/Getty Images, p. 4; EmirMemedovski/Getty Images, p. 7; Jose Luis Pelaez Inc/Getty Images, pp. 10, 21; Jacob Wackerhausen/Getty Images, p. 14; michaeljung/Getty Images, p. 18. Design element: Agunar/Shutterstock.

Cover: Witthaya Prasongsin/Getty Images.

Index

For my favorite doctor, Dr. Carl Lang —PJM

Lerner Publications Company
An imprint of Lerner Publishing Group, Inc.
241 First Avenue North
Minneapolis, MN 55401 USA

For reading levels and more information, look up this title at www.lernerbooks.com.

Main body text set in Mikado.
Typeface provided by HvD Fonts.

Editor: Annie Zheng **Designer:** Laura Otto Rinne

Library of Congress Cataloging-in-Publication Data

Names: Murphy, Patricia J., 1963- author.
Title: First visit to the doctor with Elmo / Patricia J. Murphy.
Description: Minneapolis : Lerner Publications, [2025] | Series: Sesame Street firsts | Includes bibliographical references and index. | Audience: Ages 4–8 | Audience: Grades K–1 | Summary: "Visiting the doctor is important to keep our bodies healthy. Join Elmo and his Sesame Street friends as they learn what to expect from a doctor visit"— Provided by publisher.
Identifiers: LCCN 2024037522 (print) | LCCN 2024037523 (ebook) | ISBN 9798765661024 (library binding) | ISBN 9798765684801 (paperback) | ISBN 9798765680810 (epub)
Subjects: LCSH: Children—Medical examinations—Juvenile literature. | Children—Preparation for medical care—Juvenile literature. | Physicians—Juvenile literature.
Classification: LCC RJ50.5 .M876 2025 (print) | LCC RJ50.5 (ebook) | DDC 618.92/0075—dc23/eng/20241104
LC record available at https://lccn.loc.gov/2024037522
LC ebook record available at https://lccn.loc.gov/2024037523

Manufactured in the United States of America
1-1011807-53657-10/22/2024